ESPIONAGE BLACK BOOK NINE

In this series of technical monographs:

ESPIONAGE BLACK BOOK NINE:

Secret Police Explained

Henry W. Prunckun

Bibliologica Press

Espionage Black Book Nine:
Secret Police Explained
by Henry W. Prunckun

ISBN 978-0-6456209-9-3

A catalogue record for this
book is available from the
NATIONAL LIBRARY OF AUSTRALIA
National Library of Australia

Bibliologica Press
P.O. Box 656
Unley, South Australia, 5061
Australia

CONTENTS

— CHAPTER ONE —

Introduction

OBJECTIVES, FOCUS, AND INSIGHTS

T his book provides a comprehensive explanation of secret police organizations across different sociopolitical contexts. Through a blend of historical examination, case studies, ethical discussions, and exploratory research, the book aims to answer important questions such as: What are the origins of secret police? How do they function within different kinds of political systems? What ethical and moral considerations surround their existence and operations? How do they impact the societies in which they operate?

Readers can expect to learn about the issues that go into defining secret police agencies. They will be introduced to the historical evolution of these organizations and how their roles have changed over time. They will gain insight into the philosophical and legal frameworks that either justify or condemn the existence of secret police.

Through a case study approach,[1] readers will be able to understand the tactics and strategies employed by these

---

1. The type of case study approach used in this technical monograph following a real-life contextual approach. This method is considered to be able to provide a more comprehensive understanding of the phenomena than other cases study methodologies.

1

agencies and the cultural, psychological, and financial aspects of their operations.

Finally, the book seeks to provide a balanced perspective by exploring the criticisms and downsides of secret police (i.e., authoritarian regimes) as well as the arguments favoring having such organizations as part of a country's security apparatus (i.e., democratic nations).

The book hopes to equip readers to understand the role of secret police in the modern world. This understanding will better position readers to engage in discussions and reasoned judgments about the moral, ethical, and practical implications of secret police activities.

DEFINING SECRET POLICE

The term *secret police* is imbued with layers of meaning. These interpretations evoke a range of emotions that can differ depending on the context in which it is used. At its most fundamental level, the term refers to a specialized branch of a law enforcement or intelligence agency that operates in secrecy, often with limited accountability to external oversight mechanisms. However, delving deeper into the term reveals a tapestry of connotations encompassing historical, ethical, and sociopolitical dimensions.[2]

Historically, the concept of secret police has evolved alongside the political and social changes of the times. In authoritarian regimes, secret police are synonymous with fear, coercion, and state-sanctioned violence. These agencies often act as the strong arm of the government,

---

2. Thomas Plate and Andrea Darvi, *Secret Police: An Inside Story of an International Network* (London: Robert Hale, 1981).

working to suppress dissent, monitor citizens, and eliminate threats to the ruling power, whether real or perceived.

Yet, in an egalitarian context, secret police might be considered necessary components of statecraft, responsible for maintaining order, conducting high-level investigations, and safeguarding national security.[3] The historical narratives surrounding secret police create a foundation for differing interpretations shaped by national history and collective memory.

From a legal standpoint, the role of secret police can vary based on the laws and regulations that govern them. In open societies with more robust legal frameworks, the term may imply a certain level of oversight and restrictions, although this is not always true. In controlling regimes, legal ambiguity often enables these agencies to operate outside the boundaries of what is publicly acceptable or lawful, contributing to a more nefarious interpretation of the term.

Ethically, the term *secret police* is fraught with moral complexities. On the one hand, proponents argue that secret police fulfill a critical role in protecting national interests, countering terrorism, and maintaining societal stability. On the other hand, critics contend that these organizations' secret and unaccountable nature creates conditions ripe for human rights abuses, including illegal detentions, torture, and extrajudicial killings. These ethical debates serve to polarize further interpretations of

---

3. David Wright-Nevilla, "The Australian Intelligence Community," in Daniel Baldino, editor, *Democratic Oversight of the Intelligence Services* (Sydney: The Federation Press, 2010), pp. 39–43.

what the term means and the value judgments associated with it.

Socio-politically, the term mirrors the zeitgeist of public sentiment towards governance and authority. The term might be stripped of some of its darker connotations in societies where trust in institutions is high. Conversely, in environments where mistrust towards the government dominates, the term *secret police* is laced with notions of state-sponsored oppression.

SECRET POLICE VERSUS TRADITIONAL LAW ENFORCEMENT

Secret police occupy a unique role within the larger landscape of a nation's security and intelligence apparatus. Unlike traditional law enforcement agencies, which operate within a clearly defined set of legal guidelines and focus on maintaining public order and safety, secret police organizations work in the shadows and have far more nebulous and expansive mandates. Their functions include counterterrorism, counterespionage, anti-sedition, and countermanding foreign interference.

Traditional law enforcement agencies, such as municipal police departments, are public-facing organizations tasked with crime prevention, investigation, and community engagement. They are bound by laws that govern their interactions with citizens, including how and when they can make arrests, collect evidence, or use force.[4] Their activities are transparent and held accountable through multiple oversight mechanisms such

---

4. Trevor Jones, Tim Newburn, and David J. Smith, *Democracy and Policing* (London: Policy Studies Institute, 1994).

as internal affairs units, civilian review boards, and judicial processes.

In contrast, secret police organizations operate with opacity. While they may share some overlapping functions—such as investigative work—their remit extends into realms that go beyond criminal justice. They can be involved in shaping political narratives, infiltrating opposition groups, and even conducting extrajudicial activities that would be illegal or unethical for conventional law enforcement agencies.[5] In nations that do not have a strong democracy, secret police can also be insulated from the oversight mechanisms that govern traditional law enforcement, making their actions more difficult to scrutinize.

SOCIETAL IMPLICATIONS

In studying secret police, it is important to ground our understanding in the broader societal implications inherent in their existence. The presence of secret police invariably impacts public life's psychological, trust-based, and civil liberties aspects.

Psychologically, secret police create an omnipresent sense of surveillance and, hence, uncertainty. This pervasive surveillance fosters a climate of fear and paranoia as individuals become wary of expressing dissent views of the government or engaging in activities that could be perceived as subversive.

The fear of being watched and potentially punished can lead to self-censorship, where people limit their freedom

---

5. Carol Ackroyd, Karen Margolis, Jonathan Rosenhead, and Tim Shallice, *The Technology of Political Control, Second Edition* (London: Pluto Press, 1980).

of expression and behavior, not out of direct coercion but due to the internalized presence of an unseen observer. This phenomenon can alter social interactions and individual behavior, leading to a more conformist and less vibrant ideas-based society.

Furthermore, the presence of secret police erodes public trust, both in fellow citizens and in the governing bodies. In closed societies, there can be a constant suspicion that anyone could be an informant, straining interpersonal relationships and community bonds.[6]

Once eroded, trust—a fundamental element of social cohesion—can lead to a fragmented society where collective action and mutual aid become challenging. Additionally, the use of secret police by the state to monitor and control its citizens often leads to a widespread distrust in government and its institutions. This distrust undermines the state's legitimacy and can lead to increased political instability, ironically needing more secret policing.

Lastly, the impact of secret police on civil liberties cannot be overstated. In their pursuit of state security and suppression of dissent, secret police in less than democratic nations often operate outside the bounds of legal and ethical norms. These actions go a long way in curtailing civil liberties such as the right to privacy, freedom of speech, and freedom of assembly. An unchecked power of secret police can result in abuses of power by acts such as arbitrary detention, torture, and extrajudicial punishments, all of which have a chilling

---

6. Paul Cowan, Nick Egleson, and Nat Hentoff, with Barbara Herbert and Robert Wall, *State Secrets: Police Surveillance in America* (New York: Holt, Rinehart and Winston, 1974).

effect on society. These practices not only violate individual rights but also undermine the rule of law, which is a cornerstone of democratic societies.

However, even democratic countries can suffer such abuses. Take, as an example, the case in the of the FBI. Although its abuses *never* reached the levels of arbitrary detention, torture, and extrajudicial punishments, they did involve illegal surveillance targeting people who differed with the political views of the outlook of the day. These abuses are documented in detail in several government reports, but in particular, the final report into the intelligence activities by the U.S. Senate Select Committee.

The final report of the *United States Senate Select Committee to Study Governmental Operations with Respect to Intelligence Activities*, commonly referred to as the Church Committee after its chairman, Senator Frank Church, in 1976, presented a comprehensive examination of the activities of U.S. intelligence agencies, including the Federal Bureau of Investigation.[7]

It exposed a range of covert operations and tactics employed by the FBI, which were often conducted without appropriate legal oversight or public accountability. One of the most notable revelations was the COINTELPRO program, a series of covert and often illegal activities conducted by the FBI aimed at

---

7. U.S. Senate Select Committee to Study Governmental Operations with Respect to Intelligence Activities, *Final Report: Intelligence Activities and the Rights of Americans* (Washington, D.C.: 94th Cong., 2nd sess., 1976), Report No. 94–755.

surveilling, infiltrating, discrediting, and disrupting domestic political organizations.

These operations were not only directed against perceived threats to national security but also targeted groups and individuals, including civil rights organizations and leaders, feminist groups, socialist organizations, and even individuals deemed to be subversive for their political beliefs.

The report also highlighted the FBI's extensive use of unauthorized wiretaps, the planting of informants, and the compilation of secret dossiers on thousands of American citizens, often without any legitimate law enforcement purpose. This level of surveillance and infiltration was found to be intrusive and frequently conducted in violation of constitutional rights, particularly the First Amendment rights of free speech and association.

By way of example, take one of the many dozens of cases cited in the Chuch Committee report about fifteen U.S. Navy mess attendants who, in 1941, complained of racial discrimination. The FBI started an intelligence investigation into the NAACP,[8] representing the men, that lasted at least twenty-five years (i.e., until 1966).

The investigation expanded to encompass NAACP chapters in cities across the nation. Although the ostensible purpose of this investigation was to determine if there was 'Communist infiltration' of the NAACP, the

---

8. The National Association for the Advancement of Colored People (NAACP) is a civil rights organization in the United States, formed in 1909. It is one of the oldest and most influential civil rights organizations in the nation. Its objective is to ensure the political, educational, social, and economic equality of rights of all persons and to eliminate racial hatred and racial discrimination.

investigation constituted a long-term monitoring of the NAACP's wholly lawful political activities by FBI informants.[9]

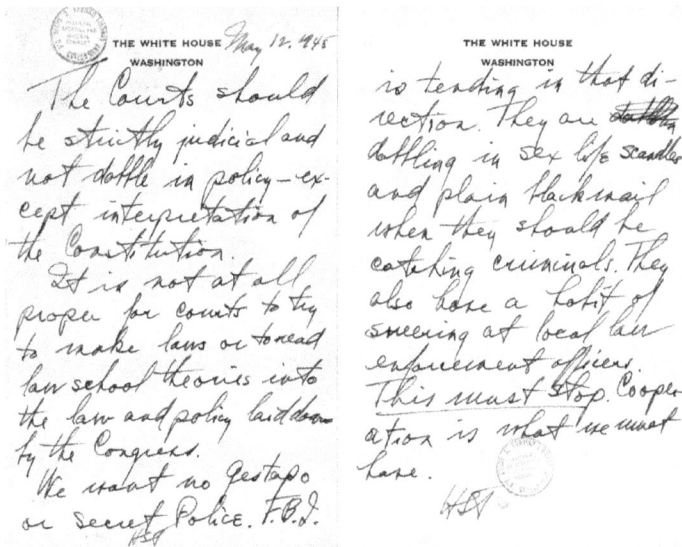

Figure 1—President Harry S. Truman's *Longhand Note* of May 12, 1945, expressed concern about Hoover's FBI tactics.

The Church Committee's findings underscored the lack of effective oversight and control over the FBI's intelligence activities. It demonstrated how unchecked executive power and the absence of stringent legislative or judicial oversight facilitated a culture within the FBI where constitutional safeguards were frequently ignored.

Yet, the Church Committee's revelations were nothing new in government circles. In personal documents penned in 1945, President Harry S. Truman expressed his view that the Federal Bureau of Investigation, led by Director J.

---

9. U.S. Senate Select Committee, *Final Report*, 179.

Edgar Hoover, had evolved into a form of secret police. He drew parallels between the FBI's operations and those of the Gestapo.[10]

> ...We want no Gestapo or Secret Police. F.B.I. is tending in that direction. They are dabbling in sex life scandals [sic] and plain blackmail when they should be catching criminals. They also have a habit of sneering at local law enforcement officers. This must stop. Cooperation is what we must have.[11]

---

10. The Gestapo, an abbreviation of *Geheime Staatspolizei*, meaning "Secret State Police," was the official secret police of Nazi Germany. Established in 1933, shortly after Adolf Hitler's rise to power, the Gestapo played a central role in the enforcement of the totalitarian policies of the Nazi regime and became a symbol of state repression.

11. Harry S. Truman, *Longhand Note of President Harry S. Truman, May 12, 1945*, President's Secretary's Files, Folder: May 12, 1945.

— CHAPTER TWO —

Historical Overview

CRUCIAL ERAS AND SOCIOPOLITICAL CONTEXT

The historical roots of secret police are deeply intertwined with the evolution of state power and the need for political control, spanning several key periods and sociopolitical climates. Their inception can be traced back to ancient times, with early examples evident in empires where rulers sought to consolidate power and suppress dissent.

During the Roman Empire, the Frumentarii, initially tasked with grain supply and postal service, evolved into agents used by emperors to spy on and suppress political opponents. This early form of secret policing was characterized by its use for personal and political gain by those in power, setting a precedent for future secret police organizations.[12]

The concept further developed in the medieval period, particularly within the Byzantine Empire. The notorious Byzantine secret police, known as the Varangian Guard, maintained the emperor's control over his subjects and silenced opposition. These practices of surveillance and control were not unique to Byzantium. They were mirrored in various forms across different medieval states,

---

12. Heidi Wendt, *At The Temple Gates: The Religion Of Freelance Experts In The Roman Empire* (New York: Oxford University Press, 2016).

reflecting the universal desire of rulers to maintain their grip on power.

In modern history, the establishment of the Oprichnina by Ivan the Terrible in 16th-century Russia marked a significant evolution in the function and structure of secret police. This force was used to consolidate the Tsar's power, control the nobility, and suppress rebellion, using methods that would become hallmarks of later secret police organizations: espionage, confiscation of property, and brutal repression.

The twentieth century witnessed the most notorious and sophisticated development of secret police organizations, shaped by the sociopolitical climates of totalitarian regimes. The Gestapo in Nazi Germany,[13] the KGB in the former Soviet Union,[14] and the Stasi in what was once East Germany[15] are prominent examples. These organizations were characterized by their extensive use of surveillance, propaganda, and terror to maintain the state's control over its citizens. Their operations were marked by systematic violations of human rights, including arbitrary arrests, torture, and executions.

The Gestapo, the KGB, and the Stasi arose from distinct sociopolitical climates that facilitated their emergence and defined their operations.

---

13. Carsten Dams and Michael Stolle, translated by Charlotte Ryland, *The Gestapo: Power and Terror in the Third Reich* (Oxford: Oxford University Press, 2014).
14. Ilya Dzhirkvelov, Secret Servant: My Life in the KGB and the Soviet Elite (London: Collins,1987).
15. Jens Gieseke, *The History of the Stasi: East Germany's Secret Police, 1945–1990* (New York: Berghahn, 2014).

In Nazi Germany, the Gestapo was a product of the dictatorial regime of Adolf Hitler. The sociopolitical climate was characterized by the Nazis' desire to consolidate power and implement their ideology across Germany. This era was marked by the suppression of political dissent, persecution of minorities, and the extensive use of propaganda. The Gestapo played a crucial role in enforcing Nazi policies, conducting surveillance, and eliminating opposition, all under the guise of maintaining state security and purity.[16]

The KGB's emergence in the Soviet Union resulted from the Communist Party's need to maintain its control over the vast and diverse territories of the USSR. The sociopolitical climate during the Soviet era was dominated by the Communist Party's pursuit of ideological conformity and control over all aspects of life. The KGB functioned as a tool for the party to monitor, suppress, and eliminate any perceived threats to its authority, including political dissidents, intellectuals, and even members of the party itself.[17]

In East Germany, the Stasi was formed in the aftermath of World War II, during the period of Soviet influence in Eastern Europe. The sociopolitical climate in East Germany was defined by the Cold War tensions and the East German government's efforts to establish a socialist state aligned with the Soviet Union. The Stasi became one of the most effective and repressive secret police

---

16. Helmut Krausnick, Hans Buchheim, Martin Broszat and Hans-Adolf Jacobsen, translated from the German by Rihard Barry, Marian Jackson, and Dorothy Lang, *Anatomy of the SS State* (New York: Walker and Company, 1968).
17. Ronald Hingley, *The Russian Secret Police* (Melbourne: Hutchinson 1970).

organizations, known for its extensive network of informants and its invasive methods of surveillance. Its goal was to ensure the Communist Party's dominance and suppress opposition or dissent.[18]

These secret police organization were not the only ones. Prior to the Second World War, Japan's state of policing and surveillance showed greater similarities with the police states of Germany in the eighteenth and nineteenth centuries than with its counterparts of the same era, such as Nazi Germany, Fascist Italy under Mussolini, and the Soviet Union under Stalin.

In the 1930s, Japan operated a secret police organization, the Tokkō, or Special Higher Police. This unit was primarily tasked with internal security and counterintelligence. Established to combat the perceived threats of communism and socialist movements, the Tokkō played a crucial role in enforcing state ideology and suppressing political dissent. It functioned under the authority of the Ministry of Home Affairs. It was notorious for its surveillance, arrest, and torture of political opponents, especially those involved in leftist activities or labor movements.

The Tokkō's activities reflected Japan's broader authoritarian and militaristic trends during this period, as the government sought to unify the country under imperial rule and prepare for expansionist military campaigns. This secret police force was instrumental in maintaining internal security. However, it did so at the expense of civil liberties and political freedoms, operating with

---

18. John O. Koehler, *Stasi: The Untold Story of the East German Secret Police* (Boulder, CO: Westview Press, 2000).

considerable autonomy and often using extralegal measures.[19]

CATALYSTS IN THE EVOLUTION OF SECRET POLICE

The formation and dissolution of secret police organizations were often precipitated by events like revolutions, wars, or ideological shifts, which catalyzed changes in political power and social order.

Revolutions, in particular, can lead to the establishment of new secret police forces as a means for the revolutionary regime to consolidate power and suppress counter-revolutionary elements. For instance, the Bolshevik Revolution in Russia led to the formation of the Cheka, a secret police force aimed at rooting out enemies of the new Soviet state.

Similarly, ideological revolutions, such as the rise of fascism in Nazi Germany, paved the way for the Gestapo to enforce the new autocratic regime's policies by suppressing any form of dissent.

Conversely, the end of wars or the collapse of political regimes can lead to the dissolution of secret police organizations. The fall of the Soviet Union, for example, resulted in the disbandment of the KGB, as the new political climate aimed for greater openness and reform.

In Germany, post-World War II, the dismantling of the Nazi regime led to the dissolution of the Gestapo, with its functions and personnel being absorbed into new systems or subjected to de-Nazification efforts.

---

19. EliseTipton, *Japanese Police State: Tokkō in Interwar Japan* (North Sydney: Allen & Unwin, 1990).

These shifts often reflect broader societal changes and the reconfiguration of power structures. The emergence or disappearance of secret police is linked to the political and ideological tides shaping a nation's history, underscoring the dynamic relationship between state power, societal change, and control and surveillance mechanisms.

SECRET POLICE ACROSS DIFFERENT REGIMES

A comparative overview of secret police organizations from various parts of the world offers a global perspective on how these agencies functioned under different regimes.

The secret police in Libya under Muammar Gaddafi's regime were pivotal in sustaining his long-standing rule. This assertion necessitates a more detailed look at the nature, methods, and impacts of these covert forces.[20]

The function of the Libyan secret police, which operated in the shadows of Gaddafi's government, was to suppress dissent and opposition. The tactics employed were as diverse as they were invasive. Surveillance was omnipresent, extending not just to known dissidents but also to the general population. This monitoring created an atmosphere of fear and mistrust, effectively stifling public discourse and any potential for organized resistance.[21]

Arbitrary detention and torture were other methods used. Individuals suspected of opposing Gaddafi's rule were detained without due process, with many subjected

---

20. Rejeanne Lacroix, "From Authoritarianism to Fragmentation and Possible New Beginnings," in Ryan Scaffer, editor, *The Handbook of African Intelligence Cultures* (Lanham: MD: Rowman & Littlefield, 2023).

21. Geoff L. Simons, *Libya and the West: From Independence to Lockerbie* (Oxford: Bloomsbury Academic, 2003).

to severe and inhumane treatment. These practices served a dual purpose: they removed active opponents from the public sphere and sent a clear, intimidating message to anyone considering dissent.

The psychological impact of these methods on Libyan society was profound. The fear of surveillance and the threat of detention and torture created a culture of self-censorship, where people were hesitant to express their views, associate freely, or engage in political activities. This environment undermined the development of civil society and political pluralism, two elements critical for a functioning democracy.[22]

Moreover, the actions of the secret police contributed to the international isolation of Libya. Reports of human rights abuses drew widespread condemnation from the global community, impacting Libya's relationships with other nations and international organizations.

The secret police in Iran under the current regime, guided by the religious leadership, presents a different yet equally complex political landscape compared to the Shah's era. This shift in governance from a monarchical to a theocratic system changed the structure, objectives, and methods of Iran's secret policing.

The Islamic Revolutionary Guard Corps (IRGC) and the Ministry of Intelligence and Security (MOIS) are two institutions that function akin to secret police in contemporary Iran. These organizations, rooted in the

---

22. Ephraim Kahana and Muhammad Suwaed, *Historical Dictionary of Middle Eastern Intelligence* (Lanham, MD: Scarecrow Press, 2009),

theocratic ideology of the regime, play a central role in maintaining its power and suppressing dissent.[23]

The IRGC, established after the 1979 Iranian Revolution, has evolved into a powerful military and political entity. Its mandate extends beyond conventional military duties, including internal security involvement.

The Basij, a paramilitary volunteer militia operating under the IRGC, is particularly notable for suppressing internal dissent. The Basij have been instrumental in cracking down on protests and demonstrations, often using excessive force. They are known for their presence in universities, workplaces, and neighborhoods, where they monitor and report on activities deemed contrary to the regime's values.

Conversely, the MOIS is engaged in intelligence gathering, counterintelligence, and surveillance. It targets a spectrum of threats, from political activists and human rights defenders to ethnic and religious minorities. The MOIS is notorious for its extensive use of informants and sophisticated surveillance techniques. Like SAVAK[24] under the Shah, it employs harsh interrogation methods, including torture, to extract confessions or intimidate opponents.

---

23. David D. Silinsky, *Empire of Terror: Iran's Islamic Revolutionary Guard Corps* (Lincoln, NE: Photomac Books, 2021).
24. SAVAK, which stands for Sazman-e Ettela'at va Amniyat-e Keshvar, was the secret police, domestic security and intelligence service established in Iran during the reign of Mohammad Reza Shah Pahlavi. It was created in 1957 with the objective to ensure the security of the Shah's regime.

The actions of these organizations have implications for civil liberties and human rights in Iran. The pervasive surveillance and brutal crackdowns on dissent create an atmosphere of fear, limiting freedom of expression and association. These practices not only stifle political opposition but also inhibit the formation of a robust civil society, crucial for democratic engagement.

In Cuba, the role of the secret police has been central to the state's apparatus since the 1959 revolution, reflecting a distinct approach to maintaining governmental control. This aspect of Cuban governance demands an exploration of the specific structures, tactics, and impacts of the secret police on Cuban society.

The Cuban secret police, known as the Department of State Security (DSE),[25] have played a pivotal role in the post-revolutionary state. Like other secret police organizations, their operations are characterized by an extensive network of informants and a comprehensive surveillance system. This network permeates various levels of Cuban society, from neighborhoods and workplaces to academic institutions, ensuring widespread monitoring of potential dissent.[26]

One of the defining features of the Cuban secret police is their focus on preventive surveillance. Rather than just targeting known dissidents, they aim to identify and neutralize potential opposition before it can manifest into

---

25. The Department of State Security is a part of the Ministry of Interior. It is not to be confused with Cuba's Intelligence Directorate (DI), commonly known as G2. The Intelligence Directorate is responsible for all foreign intelligence collection.

26. Leo Casey, "Still the 'Ashes of the Old': Human and Labor Rights in Castro's Cuba," in *Dissent*, Volume 58, Number 1, Winter 2011, pp. 23–26.

active resistance. This approach involves monitoring individuals who express critical views of the government, even if they do not engage in explicit anti-government activities.

The DSE employs various tactics to suppress opposition. These include using "acts of repudiation," where government supporters publicly denounce and harass perceived dissidents, often leading to social ostracism. Additionally, the secret police are known to conduct arbitrary detentions, often without formal charges or due process, as a method of intimidation and control.

> As such, Cuba's intelligence culture is unlike any other intelligence community on the planet, and despite overt changes of Cuban leadership in 2021, it will likely remain both prolific within its realm and decidedly undemocratic in nature.[27]

The psychological impact of these tactics on a populace is considerable. The knowledge that one could be watched and reported on breeds a climate of caution and self-censorship, limiting criticism of the government. This atmosphere undermines the development of an open civil society.[28]

These examples illustrate the contexts in which secret police operate. Although none share a standard model or culture, they share common themes of suppressing dissent, controlling information, and using fear to

---

27. Brendan J. de Brun, "Cuba," in Florina Cristiana Matei, Carolyn Halladay, and Eduardo E. Estevez, editors, *The Handbook of Latian American and Caribbean Intelligence Cultures* (Lanham, MD: Rowman & Littlefiwld, 2022), p. 308.

28. Marius Mehrl, and Ioannis Choulis, "Secret Police Organizations and State Repression," in *The Journal of Conflict Resolution*, 2023.

maintain the ruling regime's power. This is because "Intelligence services ostensibly serve the needs of government and society. Since governmental and societal conditions, objectives, and requirements vary, they shape intelligence cultures in different ways."[29] Nevertheless, this cursory comparison underscores the methods and impacts of secret police organizations in different sociopolitical environments globally.

---

29. Ryan Shaffer, "Introduction," in Ryan Shaffer, editor, *The Handbook of Asian Intelligence Cultures* (Lanham, MD: Rowman & Littlefield, 2019), p. xvii.

— CHAPTER THREE —

Philosophy and Law in Secret Policing

THEORIES AND PHILOSOPHIES

At the core of the philosophical underpinnings of secret police is the concept of state security and the protection of national interests. Often, the formation of such organizations is premised on the consideration that the state possesses a fundamental right to safeguard its existence, sovereignty, and internal stability. This view is rooted in the philosophy of statism, where the state is the central authority that maintains social order and national integrity. Secret police, in this interpretation, are instrumental in defending the state against internal threats, be they real or perceived.[30]

However, the philosophy underlying secret police organizations is not monolithic and varies depending on the type of governance and a nation's historical and cultural context. In authoritarian regimes, for instance, the secret police function as an apparatus to consolidate power, suppress dissent, and maintain the status quo.

This function is underpinned by a philosophy that prioritizes the survival and dominance of the ruling elite over individual freedoms and democratic principles. Here, the secret police are seen as necessary to control and

---

30. Ronald Hingley, *The Russian Secret Police: Muscovite, Imperial Russian and Soviet Political Security Operations, 1565–1970* (London: Routledge, 2021).

eliminate opposition, often justified through national unity and stability propaganda.[31]

In contrast, in democracies, where secret police or equivalent organizations exist, their role and justification are typically constrained by legal and ethical considerations. The philosophical underpinning in such contexts is often a balance between individual liberties and collective security. The existence of secret police in democracies is usually accompanied by rigorous legal frameworks and oversight mechanisms to prevent abuse of power and to align police operations with democratic values and human rights.

Nevertheless, the role of the secret police has been a subject of philosophical debate. Some critics have argued that the existence of secret police is antithetical to democratic principles. They point out the potential for abuse of power, lack of transparency, and the erosion of civil liberties, as was demonstrated in the Church Committee investigation.[32] On the other hand, proponents argue that such organizations must address threats that conventional law enforcement agencies are ill-equipped to handle, especially in the context of complex modern security challenges.

The justification for the existence of secret police often stems from theories emphasizing state security and stability. In this view, the secret police are necessary to protect the state from internal threats and preserve national

31. Katherine Verdery, *Secrets and Truths: Ethnography in the rchves of Romania's Secret Police* (Budapest: Central European University Press, 2014).

32. U.S. Senate Select Committee, *Final Report*.

order. This perspective can be found in *realpolitik*,[33] a theory of pragmatic governance where the maintenance of state power and stability takes precedence over ideological considerations. In authoritarian regimes, this justification is frequently used to legitimize the suppression of dissent and the strict control of information under the pretext of preserving national unity and preventing chaos.[34]

However, these justifications are met with critiques from various theoretical perspectives. From a liberal democratic standpoint, the existence of secret police is often viewed as a threat to individual liberties and democratic principles. Theories based on human rights and constitutionalism have posited that the unchecked power of secret police poses a danger to the rule of law, transparency, and accountability. The potential for abuse, privacy infringement, and the suppression of lawful dissent are vital concerns.[35]

Also, critical theories, such as those emerging from Marxist and post-colonial perspectives, often view the secret police as instruments of class domination or colonial oppression. These theories argue that secret police are used by the ruling classes or colonial powers to

---

33. Ira S. Cohen, *Realpolitik: Theory and Practice* (Encino, CA: Dickenson, 1975).

34. Jonathan R. Adelman, editor, *Terror and Communist Politics : The Role of the Secret Police in Communist States* (Boulder, CO: Westview Press, 1984).

35. *Political Imprisonment in Cuba : A Special Report from Amnesty International* (Washington, D.C.: Cuban-American National Foundation, 1987).

maintain their dominance by suppressing progressive movements and silencing voices of resistance.

Another perspective is offered by security studies scholars, who examine the role of secret police in the context of national and international security landscapes. These theories often contend with the challenges of non-state actors, terrorists, organized criminals, and freelance spies, arguing that traditional law enforcement is insufficient to address such threats. Here, secret police are considered a necessary component of a comprehensive security strategy.

In contrast, theories of governance and public administration scrutinize the efficiency and effectiveness of secret police. They question whether the benefits of having such an organization outweigh the costs regarding resources and the impact on public trust and governance quality.[36]

In this context, efficiency pertains to how well secret police achieve their objectives with the least resource expenditure. It involves assessing whether these organizations accomplish their goals using optimal financial, human, and technological resources. The effectiveness of the secret police is measured by the extent to which they contribute to the stability and security of a state. This includes evaluating their success in detecting and neutralizing threats, maintaining public order, and supporting the government's broader policy goals.

---

36. Juan J. Linz, *Totalitarian and Authoritarian Regimes* (Boulder, CO: Lynne Rienner Publishers, 2000).

CRITICAL CRIMINOLOGY'S VIEW

Critical criminology is a theoretical perspective that views crime as a product of social and economic inequality, focusing on how power structures and societal inequalities influence laws, criminal behavior, and the justice system. It challenges traditional understandings of crime and justice, emphasizing the role of societal factors and power dynamics in shaping criminality and crime responses.

A critical criminologist might view secret police agencies through a lens that scrutinizes the interplay of power, social inequality, and state control. Secret police agencies, often operating covertly and outside the usual bounds of legal and ethical accountability, would be perceived as instruments of the state used to maintain and enforce the existing power structures, particularly those that serve the interests of the ruling elite or dominant political class.[37]

From this perspective, the existence and operations of secret police are not merely about law enforcement or national security; they are deeply embedded in the socio-political fabric and serve to protect the status quo. Critical criminologists might argue that secret police agencies are used by those in power to suppress dissent, control marginalized populations, and perpetuate systemic inequalities. This viewpoint posits that such agencies play a key role in upholding the ruling class's interests by employing surveillance, intimidation, and even coercion against those who challenge the established order.

---

37. Phil Scraton and Kathryn Chadwick, "The Theoretical and Political Priorities of Critical Criminology," in Kevin Stenson and David Cowell, editors, *The Politics of Crime Control* (London: Sage, 1991), pp. 161–185.

Additionally, critical criminologists would be particularly attentive to the methods employed by secret police agencies. These methods often include surveillance, infiltration, and the disruption of subversive groups. In this view, the targeting and criminalization of specific groups or individuals by secret police are seen as reflective of broader societal inequalities and power dynamics. This approach would suggest that the activities of secret police are not neutral but are heavily influenced by the socio-political context, with certain ideologies, social movements, or communities being disproportionately targeted based on their perceived threat to the status quo.[38]

Furthermore, critical criminology would also consider the impact of secret police activities on society. This includes the erosion of civil liberties, the perpetuation of community fear and mistrust, and the broader implications for democracy and social justice. The secretive and often unaccountable nature of these agencies would be a significant concern, highlighting issues of transparency, legality, and the potential for abuse of power.[39]

LEGAL FRAMEWORKS AND OVERSIGHT

At the domestic level, in open societies, the legal framework governing secret police activities is typically enshrined in national legislation. This legislation outlines the permissible scope of secret police activities, the methods they may employ, and the conditions under which they operate.

---

38. Richard Quinney, *The Social Relaity of Crime* (Boston: Little, Brown and Company, 1970).
39. Paula Ugwudike, *An Introduction to Critical Criminology* (Bristol, UK: Policy Press, 2015).

Critical aspects of these laws often include provisions for surveillance, detention, and intelligence collection, as well as safeguards against the abuse of power. For instance, laws may specify the need for judicial warrants for certain types of surveillance or establish guidelines for treating detainees to prevent human rights violations. Additionally, domestic legal frameworks often define the accountability mechanisms to which secret police are subject, including oversight by legislative bodies, judiciary, or independent watchdogs. These mechanisms ensure that the secret police operate within the law and are held accountable for overreach or misconduct.

Internationally, the secret police activities of free nations are also subject to various legal instruments, particularly those about humanitarian law. International conventions such as the *International Covenant on Civil and Political Rights* (ICCPR)[40] and the *Convention Against Torture and Other Cruel, Inhuman or Degrading Treatment or Punishment*[41] provide guidelines on treating individuals and protecting civil liberties, which secret police agencies are obliged to respect. These international standards serve as a benchmark for evaluating the conduct of secret police and offer a framework for international scrutiny and criticism in cases of human rights violations.

The interplay between domestic and international legal frameworks creates the legal environment where secret police operate. While domestic laws provide the immediate legal basis for their activities, international laws offer an overarching framework that shapes global expectations and standards.

---

40. General Assembly (New York: United Nations, 1976).
41. General Assembly (New York: United Nations, 1987).

Compliance with international law not only aids in legitimizing the operations of secret police on the global stage but also helps prevent international censure and potential sanctions. The effective oversight of secret police is crucial in ensuring they adhere to these legal standards.

Oversight mechanisms in democracies can take various forms, including parliamentary committees, judicial review, independent regulatory bodies, and public transparency initiatives. These mechanisms are designed to provide checks and balances, preventing the misuse of power and ensuring that the activities of secret police are consistent with legal norms and public interest.[42]

Parliamentary Committees. A prominent example is the Intelligence and Security Committee (ISC) in the United Kingdom. This committee is composed of Members of Parliament. It is responsible for examining the British intelligence agencies' policy, administration, and expenditure, including activities that may involve secret police functions.

The ISC operates within the framework of parliamentary oversight, providing a layer of accountability by scrutinizing the actions of intelligence agencies and ensuring they comply with the law and ethical standards. It can investigate specific operations, review annual reports, and recommend policy or practice changes.

Judicial Review. The Foreign Intelligence Surveillance Court (FISC) is an example of judicial oversight in the

---

42. Tim Prenzler and Carol Ronken (2001), "Models of Police Oversight: A Critique," in *Policing and Society*, Volume 11, Number 2, 2010, pp. 151–180.

United States. Established to oversee requests for surveillance warrants against foreign spies inside the U.S. by federal law enforcement and intelligence agencies, FISC operates under the *Foreign Intelligence Surveillance Act* (FISA).

This court represents a judicial review mechanism, ensuring that surveillance activities, including those potentially carried out by secret police, adhere to legal standards and respect individual rights. The FISC's role is to balance the government's national security interests with protecting citizens' constitutional rights, particularly the Fourth Amendment right against unreasonable searches and seizures.

Independent Regulatory Bodies. The Office of the Inspector General of the Intelligence Community in the United States is an example of an independent oversight body. This office is tasked with conducting audits, investigations, inspections, and reviews of the intelligence community's activities, which could include those of secret police.[43]

Its independence from the agencies it oversees is crucial for ensuring objective and effective oversight. The Inspector General can investigate complaints of wrongdoing, conduct regular audits of agency operations, and make recommendations to improve efficiency and compliance with legal and ethical standards.

Public Transparency Initiatives. The Canadian Security Intelligence Service (CSIS) *Public Report* in Canada

---

43. Monica den Boer, "Police Oversight and Accountability in a Comparative Perspective," in Monica den Boer, editor, *Comparative Policing from a Legal Perspective* (Cheltenham, UK: Edward Elgar, 2018).

exemplifies a public transparency initiative. These annual reports provide the public with information about the activities and operations of CSIS, including its approach to national security threats, collaboration with domestic and international partners, and adherence to legal and ethical frameworks.[44]

While certain sensitive information is necessarily omitted for security reasons, these reports represent an effort to increase transparency and public accountability. By informing the public and inviting scrutiny, such transparency initiatives help build trust in secret police operations and ensure they are conducted in the public interest.

LOOPHOLES AND IMPLICATIONS

Despite pluralistic societies' efforts at transparency, much of the secret police work remains shrouded in secrecy. This lack of transparency can lead to abuses of power.

Limited Accountability. Political pressures, limited resources, and restricted access to information can hinder the ability of oversight bodies to hold secret police accountable. There is a greater risk of unchecked human rights violations when accountability is weak.

Legal and Ethical Ambiguities. The legal frameworks governing secret police activities contain ambiguities that act as loopholes that can be exploited. For instance, definitions of national security threats can be vague, allowing for overreach in surveillance and intelligence-gathering activities that infringe on privacy rights.

---

44. *The Canadian Security Intelligence Service: 2022 Public Report* (Minister of Public Safety: Ottawa, 2023).

Challenges in Balancing Security and Rights. The primary challenge in overseeing secret police activities is balancing national security interests with protecting individual rights. Human rights can sometimes be sidelined in pursuit of security, justified by the greater good argument.[45]

While existing oversight mechanisms play a crucial role in regulating the activities of secret police sovereign states, they are not without their limitations. Addressing these challenges requires continual reassessment and, where found necessary, strengthening oversight mechanisms to ensure that they are adequately resourced, independent, and can balance the imperatives of national security with the fundamental principles of justice.[46]

---

45. The "greater good argument" is a moral rationale used to justify actions that serve the welfare of the majority or society, often at the expense of certain individual rights or freedoms. The concept of the greater good, often associated with utilitarian philosophy, was most notably espoused by philosophers Jeremy Bentham and John Stuart Mill. In the context of national security, this argument supports practices like surveillance by secret police, asserting that state security and public safety are paramount. However, it is a contentious rationale because it can lead to the erosion of individual liberties.

46. Iian Berman, Ilan; Waller, J. Michael, "Introduction: The Centrality of the Secret Police," in *Dismantling Tyranny: Transitioning Beyond Totalitarian Regimes* (Lanham, MD: Rowman & Littlefield, 2006).

— CHAPTER FOUR —

Organizational Underpinnings

STRUCTURE AND ORGANIZATION

The hierarchical structures of secret police organizations are typically designed to ensure efficiency, secrecy, and control over their operations. This is axiomatic for both authoritarian states and constitutional republics. These structures resemble military or other security forces, characterized by a chain of command and specialized divisions or departments. Understanding the organizational underpinnings of secret police agencies involves examining the common elements of their structures.

Centralized Command and Control

At the top of the hierarchy is a central command. This command is typically led by a director or chief who controls the organization. This administrator is usually appointed by the state's highest authority, such as the president or prime minister, and is responsible for setting the overall strategy and policies of the organization.

The central command function is crucial for maintaining the secrecy and coherence of the organization's operations, ensuring that all actions align with the state's security objectives.[47]

---

47. John J. Dziak, Reflctions of the Counterintelligence State," in Hayden B. Peake and Samuel Halpin, editors, *In The Name*

An illustrative example of such a structure can be seen in the East German Stasi during the Cold War era. The *Ministerium für Staatssicherheit* (Ministry for State Security), commonly known as the *Stasi*, was the official state security service of the German Democratic Republic (East Germany).[48]

At the apex of the Stasi's hierarchical structure was the Minister of State Security. The highest authority in East Germany appointed this position, typically the General Secretary of the Socialist Unity Party (SED), who was effectively the leader of East Germany. The most notable of these Ministers was Erich Mielke, who served from 1957 until the fall of the Berlin Wall in 1989.

As the head of the Stasi, Mielke was responsible for setting the organization's overall strategy and policies. His role involved overseeing a vast network of agents and informers, coordinating intelligence operations, both domestically and internationally, and ensuring the security of the East German state against internal and external threats. Mielke directly reported to the top leadership of the SED, ensuring that the Stasi's activities were closely aligned with the political objectives of East Germany's ruling party.

Layers of Hierarchy

Beneath the central command, secret police organizations may have multiple layers of hierarchy. These layers can include various ranks and positions, each with specific

---

of Intelligence (Washington, D.C.: NIBC OPress, 1994), pp. 261–276.

48. Richard Popplewell, "The Stasi and the East German Revolution of 1989," in *Contemporary European History*, Volume 1, Number 1, 1992, pp. 37–63.

responsibilities and levels of authority. The hierarchy ensures that orders and information flow efficiently from the top down and that each level is accountable to the one above. This structure is designed to maintain control and discipline within the organization, reducing the risk of leaks or insubordination.

Specialized Divisions

Secret police organizations often comprise specialized divisions or departments, each focused on different aspects of intelligence and security. These include domestic surveillance, counterintelligence, international espionage, cybersecurity, countersubversion, anti-sabotage, and counterterrorism. Each division operates under the guidance of the central command but has its autonomy and expertise in its specific area. This specialization allows the organization to address various security challenges effectively.

The Ministry of State Security (MSS) of the People's Republic of China is a relevant example of a secret police organization with specialized divisions. The MSS, akin to secret police in its functions and operations, is responsible for intelligence, security, and secret police duties within China.[49]

The MSS is structured with various bureaus and departments, each dedicated to specific national security and intelligence areas. Key divisions include counterintelligence, foreign intelligence, domestic security, and cybersecurity. The counterintelligence

---

49. Alex Joske, *Spies and Lies: How China's Greatest Covert Operations Fooled the World* (London: Hardie Grant Books, 2022).

division focuses on preventing espionage activities by foreign agents within China.

The foreign intelligence division is responsible for gathering intelligence from abroad, essential for informing China's foreign policy and national security strategy. The domestic security division monitors and suppresses internal dissent, political opposition, and potential threats to the Chinese Communist Party's (CCP) authority. Additionally, the cybersecurity division addresses threats in the digital domain, protecting against cyber espionage and attacks on China's information infrastructure.[50]

These specialized units operate under the guidance of the MSS central command, which sets the overall strategy and ensures that the activities of the divisions align with the state's security objectives. This structure allows the MSS to effectively address a broad spectrum of security challenges, from internal stability to external threats, while maintaining a coordinated approach under the central leadership. The MSS's organization exemplifies how a secret police agency leverages specialized divisions to manage diverse and complex security and intelligence operations within a unified command structure.

Operational and Support Units

Operational units are the backbone of secret police activities. They are responsible for conducting surveillance, intelligence gathering, interrogations, and other field operations.

---

50. David Wise, *Tiger Trap: America's Secret Spy War with China* (Boston: Houghton Mifflin Harcourt, 2011).

In contrast, support units provide the necessary backing, such as logistics, technology, training, and administrative services. The balance between operational and support units is vital for the smooth functioning of the organization.[51]

Secrecy and Compartmentalization

A defining feature of all secret police organizations is the high level of secrecy and compartmentalization. Information is shared on a need-to-know basis, with controls on who has access to what information. This compartmentalization helps prevent the leakage of sensitive information but can also create challenges in coordination and information sharing within the organization.[52]

A noteworthy example of secrecy and compartmentalization is the KGB (*Komitet Gosudarstvennoy Bezopasnosti* or Committee for State Security) of the former Soviet Union. The KGB, which operated from 1954 until the dissolution of the Soviet Union in 1991, was known for its extensive intelligence activities, both domestically and internationally, and serves as a classic illustration of these operational principles.[53]

The KGB was structured to accommodate compartmentalized information, with various directorates and departments responsible for different areas of

51. n.a, *The Black Bag Owner's Manual: Part One, Spook Centre* (Boulder, CO: Paladin Press, 1978).

52. Hank Prunckun, *Counterintelligence Theory and Practice*, Second Edition (Lanham, MD: Rowman & Littlefield, 2019).

53. Allen W. Dulles, *The Craft of Intelligence* (New Delhi: Manas Publications, 2013), pp. 81 and 84.

intelligence and security. Information was controlled and shared only on a need-to-know basis. For instance, agents working in foreign intelligence were often unaware of the activities of their counterparts in domestic surveillance and vice versa.

Figure 2—Vladimir Putin's identity card, issued by the Stasi, reflects his time in Dresden, where he served as a liaison officer for the KGB.

This secrecy extended to the training of KGB officers, where individuals were instructed only in the specific skills and knowledge pertinent to their roles. Even within specific departments, there were further subdivisions, with agents often working in isolation to ensure that no single individual had a complete overview of operations.[54]

---

54. Vladimir Putin's (see Figure 2) tenure in the KGB, culminating as a lieutenant colonel in East Germany, provided him with experience in intelligence and surveillance, but his mid-level position would have limited his exposure to the agency's broader strategic operations. The compartmentalized nature of the KGB meant that operatives like Putin had access

Flexibility and Adaptability

While maintaining a hierarchical structure, secret police organizations exhibit a degree of flexibility and adaptability. This agility allows them to respond quickly to changing security situations and emerging threats. The ability to reorganize or create *ad hoc* units (e.g., task or strike teams) as needed is crucial for maintaining the effectiveness of these organizations.

SECRET POLICE AND GOVERNMENT BODIES

The relationship between secret police and other government bodies, including the military and intelligence agencies, is vital for the functioning of a state's security apparatus. The nature of these relationships varies depending on a country's political and legal frameworks (i.e., dictatorial vs. liberal states). However, they generally revolve around collaboration, jurisdictional boundaries, and the division of responsibilities.[55]

Secret police often work with national intelligence agencies. While there is an overlap in their roles, particularly in intelligence gathering and counterintelligence activities, each entity typically has mandates that specify operational focuses.

---

only to information pertinent to their specific roles, constraining their overall understanding of the organization's extensive operations. This background influenced his early political career, although his comprehensive knowledge of KGB strategies at the highest level would have been limited due to his rank and the secretive structure of the agency.

55. Hank Prunckun, *Methods of Inquiry for Intelligence Analysis, Third Edition* (Lanham, MD: Rowman & Littlefield, 2019).

Intelligence agencies usually concentrate on external threats and foreign intelligence collection, whereas secret police focus on internal security. The collaboration between these entities is necessary for sharing information and resources, ensuring coverage of internal and external security threats.[56] However, this relationship can also lead to challenges, such as competition for resources and jurisdictional conflicts, so harmony requires effective communication channels and a willingness to cooperate.

The relationship between secret police and the military varies depending on the country's political structure and history. In some nations, secret police work with the military, particularly in national security and defense areas.

In such instances, the secret police may be involved in counterterrorism operations, insurgency control, and the protection of state security, often leveraging the military's resources and capabilities. However, this collaboration must be carefully managed to distinguish between internal security, the primary domain of secret police, and external defense, which falls under the military's purview. The potential for power imbalances or conflicts of interest must be monitored to prevent overreach of power.

An illustrative example of secret police working with the military, particularly in national security and defense, can be found in the historical context of the Soviet Union during the Cold War era. Counterintelligence was one of

---

56. National Commission on Terrorist Attacks Upon the United States, *The 9/11 Commission Report: Final Report of the National Commission on Terrorist Attacks Upon the United States* (Washington, D.C.: Government Printing Office, 2004).

the critical roles of the KGB in conjunction with the military.

The KGB was tasked with uncovering spies and preventing espionage against the Soviet Union. This was particularly important during the Cold War, a period of intense espionage between the Soviet Union and the Western bloc. The KGB worked closely with the military to secure sensitive information and safeguard military secrets, including nuclear strategies, military technologies, and troop movements.[57]

A critical aspect of the relationship between secret police and other government bodies is the demarcation of responsibilities. Each entity must have a defined role and operational scope to prevent overlaps and conflicts. For instance, while secret police may engage in counterintelligence activities, these operations are usually distinct from those conducted by dedicated intelligence agencies. Similarly, any secret police involvement in matters typically handled by the military will likely be regulated to avoid encroaching on the military's jurisdiction.

FINANCIAL ASPECTS

The financial aspects of secret police organizations of all persuasions encompass a range of factors, including budgeting, fund allocation, and expenditure. These elements are essential for understanding how organizations operate and maintain their activities.

Due to the clandestine nature of these agencies, especially in closed societies, precise details about their

---

57. Christopher Andrew and Oleg Gordievsky, *KGB: The Inside Story* (London: Hodder & Stoughton, 1990).

financing are elusive because they are shrouded in secrecy. However, the literature on general policing[58] and intelligence topics sheds light on budgeting, funds allocation, and expenditure so that inferences can be drawn.

In democracies, the budgeting process for secret police organizations typically involves a combination of state funding and, in some cases, additional sources of revenue. The primary funding is usually allocated through the national government's budget, often under the auspices of national security or defense.

In some democracies, the government approval process for these budgets may require legislative approval. However, the exact figures and specifics of the allocations are classified.[59] In some one-party regimes, secret police may also have access to other forms of revenue, such as funds from covert operations, which can complicate the transparency and accountability of their financial operations. Covert operations can generate funds in various ways. For example, they might secretly sell arms or expropriate resources from other countries or entities (e.g., cyber theft or digital ransom). By their nature, these activities are not disclosed in the usual government spending process.

A secret police organization's strategic priorities and operational requirements determine the allocation. In all

---

58. Which is grounded in the literature concerning public sector budgeting and finance. For example, see Jay Eungha Ryo, *The Public Budgeting and Finance Primer* (London: Taylor & Francis, 2013), as one of many competent texts.
59. Victor Marchetti and John D. Marks, *The CIA and the Cult of Intelligence* (New York: Alfred A. Knopf, 1974).

organizations, the process will be guided by the need to balance the demands of different operational areas while ensuring the effectiveness and efficiency of the organization.

Expenditure by secret police organizations covers a broad range of activities. Operational expenditures can include staffing costs, surveillance and intelligence-gathering operations, maintenance of secure facilities, and specialized equipment.

Personnel costs are the most significant component of the expenditure. This aspect covers salaries, benefits, ongoing training for operatives, and support staff. Additionally, secret police organizations may incur costs related to covert operations, including payments to informants, the paraphernalia used in undercover operations, and the equipment and facilities needed for clandestine activities. In democratic nations, the secretive nature of these expenditures means they are exempt from the standard financial oversight and public disclosure requirements that apply to other government expenditures.[60]

---

60. Although, the agency's general financial position may be reported, but it will lack any specificity. For instance, see Australian Government, *Australian Security and Intelligence Organization, Annual Report, 2022–2023* (Canberra: Commonwealth of Australia, 2023).

— CHAPTER FIVE —

Methods and Sources

RECRUITMENT AND TRAINING

S ecret police agencies in non-authoritarian nations typically employ targeted recruitment strategies to attract suitable candidates. Recruitment methods vary, ranging from direct approaches in educational institutions and military establishments to covert recruitment drives. Higher education institutions, particularly those specializing in law, international relations, and languages, are often fertile grounds for recruiting future secret police agents. Military personnel are also considered prime candidates with their discipline and training. Additionally, some agencies use employment advertisements in disguise, targeting individuals with specific skill sets and backgrounds. [61]

In countries with more authoritarian regimes, recruitment can also involve scouting for individuals who have demonstrated loyalty and ideological alignment with the ruling party or government. In such cases, the recruitment process is often more opaque, emphasizing political reliability and adherence to state ideology.[62]

---

61. Christopher Andrew, *Defend the Realm: The Authorized History of MI5* (New York: Alfred A. Knopf, 2009).

62. Nicholas Eftimiades, *Chinese Intelligence Operations* (Annapolis, MD: Naval Institute Press, 1994).

The selection criteria for secret police agents are stringent. Key attributes include high intelligence, adaptability, and thinking critically and analytically. Emotional stability and psychological resilience are crucial, given the stressful and often morally complex nature of secret police work. Physical fitness and a clean legal record are typically standard requirements.

Language skills, particularly in foreign languages, are highly valued, as are skills in technology and cybersecurity in the modern era. Additionally, a certain level of discretion and the ability to work covertly are essential qualities.[63]

Secret police agencies often look for specific psychological profiles in their recruits. Candidates capable of operating with a high degree of autonomy yet able to follow orders precisely are highly sought after. The nature of secret police work in free countries, which can involve surveillance, interrogation, and, in some cases, covert operations, requires individuals who can navigate ethical and moral dilemmas while maintaining the agency's objectives.[64]

Recruits are often expected to have a strong sense of duty and loyalty, coupled with the ability to detach emotionally from their work. This psychological profile helps carry out operations that might be challenging or distressing, particularly in situations involving the surveillance of citizens or the enforcement of government policies that may infringe on individual rights.

---

63. Richard L. Holm, *The Craft We Chose: My Life in the CIA* (Mountain Lake Park, MD: Mountain Lake Press, 2011).

64. Jefferson Mack, *Running a Ring of Spies* (Boulder, CO: Paladin Press, 1996).

Once recruited, agents typically undergo rigorous training programs. These programs equip them with the necessary skills and knowledge for their roles. Training can include a range of subjects such as surveillance techniques, intelligence analysis, interrogation methods, cybersecurity, foreign languages, and understanding of laws and ethics. The intensity and duration of these training programs vary depending on the specific role and the agency's requirements.[65]

METHODS AND TACTICS

The methods and tactics employed by secret police agencies encompass various sophisticated strategies, including surveillance, infiltration, and psychological warfare, each serving distinct operational purposes.

Surveillance is a cornerstone of secret police activity, involving both physical and electronic means. Physical surveillance may include shadowing targets, monitoring their movements, and conducting stakeouts, often using disguise and covert methods to avoid detection.[66]

Electronic surveillance has become increasingly important, involving intercepting phone calls and emails and employing sophisticated equipment to bug homes and offices. Additionally, digital monitoring is crucial in the modern era, with secret police tracking social media activity and online behavior using advanced data analysis techniques.

---

65. Maloy Krishna Dhar, *Intelligence Tradecraft: Secrets of Spy Warfare* (New Delhi: Manas Publications, 2016).

66. Raymond P. Siljander, *Fundamentals of Physical Surveillance: A Guide for Uniformed and Plainclothes Personnel* (Springfield, IL: Charles C. Thomas, 1977).

Infiltration tactics are also crucial, with secret police agents often integrating into target groups or organizations under false identities to gather intelligence from within. This approach is complemented by networks of informants who provide inside information on communities or groups.[67] Secret police may also collaborate with other state agencies or foreign intelligence services to enhance their infiltration capabilities.

In dictatorial countries, psychological warfare forms a component of their methods. This process includes spreading disinformation and controlling local media stories through propaganda to shape public opinion. Intimidation and coercion are also employed, ranging from subtle psychological pressure to overt acts of violence or threats aimed at suppressing dissent and instilling fear. Additionally, secret police might create or exploit divisions within groups or societies, sowing discord to weaken opposition movements.[68]

Historical Technologies

In earlier times, secret police tactics were supported by relatively basic technology. Physical surveillance relied on human agents conducting stakeouts or shadowing targets.[69] The use of disguises and forged documents were common. For eavesdropping, simple mechanical devices

---

67. Cril Payne, *Deep Cover: An FBI Agent Infiltrates the Radical Underground* (New York: Newsweek Books, 1979).

68. Thomas Rid, *Active Measures: The Secret History of Disinformation and Political Warfare* (London: Profile Trade, 2020).

69. Maloy Krishna Dhar, *Intelligence Tradecraft: Screts of Spy Warfare* (New Delhi: Manas Publications, 2016).

like stethoscopes or thin tubes were used to listen through walls. Early wiretapping involved basic telephone tapping techniques, often requiring physical access to telephone lines.[70]

Photography played a crucial role, with secret police using concealed cameras to document individuals' activities—the development of smaller, more discreet cameras allowed agents to capture images without arousing suspicion. In terms of infiltration, forged identity papers and rudimentary listening devices hidden in rooms or objects were used to gather information.

Modern Technologies

Digital technology has revolutionized the devices at the disposal of agencies. Digital surveillance now includes sophisticated electronic eavesdropping, using a wide array of devices to intercept communications across various mediums—telephone, internet, and mobile networks. Encryption-breaking software and advanced algorithms enable agencies to sift through vast data to identify threats or gather intelligence.[71]

Cyber surveillance methods have become particularly important, with secret police using malware, spyware, and other intrusive software to monitor online activities and communications. This extends to tracking individuals' movements and activities through their digital footprints,

---

70. Ronald Hingley, *The Russian Secret Police: Muscovite, Imperial Russian, and Soviet Political Security Operations 1565–1970* (Richmond, VIC: Hutchinson, 1970).

71. Robert Wallace and H. Keith Melton, with Henry R. Schlesinger, *Spycraft: The Secret History of the CIA's Spytechs from Communism to Al-Qaeda* (New York: Dutton, 2008).

including social media activity, smartphone GPS data, and transaction records.[72]

Using drones and satellite technology for surveillance has added a new dimension, allowing secret police to monitor targets from a distance without direct human involvement. Biometric technology, including facial recognition software and fingerprint databases, has also become essential, enabling quick and accurate identification of individuals.

TECHNOLOGICAL EVOLUTION

The technological evolution in surveillance and intelligence has significantly impacted the operations of secret police agencies worldwide. Modern technologies like facial recognition, data mining, and artificial intelligence (AI) algorithms have been rapidly adopted or adapted by these organizations, enhancing their capabilities in unprecedented ways.

Facial recognition has become a pivotal method in the arsenal of secret police agencies. This technology allows identifying or verifying an individual from a digital image or video frame against a database. It is instrumental in crowd surveillance, border control, and monitoring of public spaces.[73]

In recent years, the implementation of facial recognition technology by secret police (sometimes referred to as state security agencies) in authoritarian

---

72. Brian Minick, *Facing Cyber Threats Head On* (Lanham, MD: Rowman & Littlefield, 2016).

73. Rita Matulionyte and Monika Zalnieriute, editors, *The Cambridge Handbook of Facial Recognition in the Modern State* (Cambridge, UK: Cambridge University Press, 2024).

regimes has been exemplified by China's surveillance practices, particularly in regions like Xinjiang.[74] The Chinese government has employed facial recognition technology as part of its extensive surveillance network, enabling real-time monitoring of its citizens. This technology has been reportedly used to track dissidents, identify participants in protests, and monitor Uighur Muslims and other minority groups.

The surveillance system in Xinjiang is known for its comprehensive nature, combining facial recognition with other technologies such as biometric data collection and AI-powered monitoring. This system allows for the continuous tracking and profiling of individuals, contributing to what has been described as a near-ubiquitous surveillance state.[75]

The use of such technology in Xinjiang and other parts of China has raised international concerns regarding its impact on privacy and civil liberties, as well as its role in facilitating human rights abuses.

Data mining involves extracting useful information from large datasets, a task increasingly crucial for secret police in the digital age. These agencies can uncover patterns, connections, and trends that might indicate potential security threats by analyzing vast amounts of data gathered from various sources like social media,

---

74. Clive Hamilton, *Silent Invasion: China's Influence in Australia* (Melbourne: Hardie Grant Books, 2018).

75. Cyrus A. Parsa. *Artificial Intelligence Dangers to Humanity: AI, U.S., China, Big Tech, Facial Recognition, Drones, Smart Phones, IoT, 5G, Robotics, Cybernetics, and Bio-Digital Social Program* (La Jolla, CA: The AI Organization, 2019).

telecommunications, and public records. Data mining techniques enable secret police to process and interpret large datasets quickly and accurately, facilitating more effective intelligence-gathering and decision-making processes.[76]

Artificial intelligence algorithms represent a significant leap forward in the capabilities of secret police. AI can automate complex processes of data analysis, recognizing patterns and anomalies that might elude human analysts. AI algorithms are particularly effective in processing and interpreting massive volumes of unstructured data, such as images, text, and videos, gathered from diverse sources. This capability allows secret police to predict potential security incidents, profile individuals, and make more informed strategic decisions.

Moreover, AI can enhance other technologies, like facial recognition, by improving accuracy and speed. In cybersecurity, AI algorithms identify and respond to threats more rapidly and effectively than traditional methods.

FOREIGN OPERATIONS AND INTERNATIONAL COLLABORATION

The scope of activities undertaken by democratic secret police organizations often extends beyond their national borders, encompassing foreign operations and international collaboration.[77] These overseas endeavors

---

76. Colleen McCue, *Data Mining and Predictive Analysis: Intelligence Gathering and Crime Analysis* (Boston: Elsevier, 2007).

77. Bob de Graaff and James M. Nyce, with Chelsea Locke, editors, *Handbook of European Intelligence Culture* (Lanham, MD: Rowman & Littlefield, 2016).

are crucial for fulfilling various objectives, from espionage and counterintelligence to influencing foreign politics and protecting national interests abroad.

Secret police agencies in some countries have developed extensive global reach, conducting covert operations in foreign nations (see Table 1 for a selected sample of such agencies). These operations include espionage—gathering sensitive political, economic, or military information.

They also engage in counterintelligence efforts abroad to protect their national secrets or counteract foreign intelligence operations. In many instances, these agencies operate clandestine networks of spies and informants across the globe, leveraging diplomatic cover or using non-official covers to conceal their activities.

Beyond espionage, some secret police agencies undertake covert actions to influence political outcomes in other countries. These activities range from disseminating propaganda and disinformation to more direct interventions like supporting coups, insurgencies, or opposition groups.[78] Such operations are often highly secretive and can have far-reaching implications for international relations and global geopolitics.

Collaboration with foreign intelligence and security agencies is another facet of the international operations of secret police. These collaborations can involve information sharing, joint operations, or coordinated efforts in counterterrorism and other security concerns. For instance, agencies from different countries might work together to dismantle transnational criminal

---

78. Stephen E. Pease, *Psywar: Psychological Warfare in Korea 1950–1953* (Harrisburg, PA: Stackpole Books, 1992).

networks or terrorist organizations, sharing intelligence and resources to achieve common goals.

Table 1—Secret Police International Reach

Country	Reach
Cuba	While not as extensively involved in global operations as larger agencies, Cuba has historically supported left-wing movements and governments, particularly in Latin America and Africa.
Iran	Iran's international activities have focused on gathering intelligence and conducting covert operations to advance Iran's strategic interests, counter perceived threats, and protect the regime from external and internal adversaries.
North Korea	The Reconnaissance General Bureau (RGB) of North Korea is known for its secretive and extensive network of agents. It has been implicated in various activities, including espionage, cyber warfare, and assassination plots. Its operations are primarily aimed at South Korea, Japan, and the United States, focusing on gathering intelligence, disrupting perceived enemy activities, and promoting North Korea's strategic interests.
Russia	The Russian government conducts a range of espionage activities through intelligence agencies like the SVR and GRU, including cyber operations, human intelligence (HUMINT) gathering, and efforts to influence political processes in the Five Eyes allies.

However, this collaboration is often a delicate balance of mutual interests and distrust, as nations are wary of revealing too much to potential rivals. Therefore, international intelligence collaboration is typically governed by strategic considerations, with agencies carefully managing what information they share and how they cooperate with their foreign counterparts.

The foreign operations and international collaborations of secret police agencies have various challenges and implications. For democratic nations, conducting operations on foreign soil raises legal and ethical questions, often in a grey area of international law.[79] These activities can lead to diplomatic tensions and conflicts when they are uncovered or if they infringe upon the sovereignty of other nations.[80]

The interaction of secret police agencies with their international counterparts, whether allies or adversaries, embodies a dynamic aspect of international espionage and intelligence work. These interactions involve information sharing among allies, particularly in areas like counterterrorism, where collective security is paramount. Training and exchange programs are standard, allowing agencies to share techniques and expertise in surveillance, cyber operations, and other espionage areas. Moreover,

---

79. Locke K. Johnson, "Ethics of Covert Operations," in Jan Goldman, editor, *Ethic of Spying* (Lanham, MD: Scarecrow Press, 2006), pp. 266–299.

80. Take, as an example, the leaking of operational details by Edward Snowden in 2013. Keiran Hardy and George Williams, "Terrorist, Trator, or Whistleblower?: Offences and Protections in Australia for Disclosing National Security Information," in *University of New South Wales Law Journal*, Volume 37, Number 2, pp. 784–819.

there is usually an effort to align policies and strategies to address common security challenges more effectively, as was found as far back as 1975 by the Commission on CIA Activities Within the United States:

> Most of the assistance rendered to state and local law enforcement agencies by the CIA has been no more than an effort to share with law enforcement authorities the benefits of new methods, techniques, and equipment developed or used by the agency. In view of ... recent statutory changes, assistance is now being provided to state and local agencies by the FBI.[81]

Conversely, interactions with adversarial nations are markedly different, focusing predominantly on counterintelligence operations. These aim to thwart foreign espionage activities, identify and neutralize spies, and safeguard sensitive information. Secret police agencies may also use disinformation campaigns and psychological operations to manipulate public perception and influence political outcomes in adversary countries. Additionally, covert operations, ranging from intelligence gathering to sabotage or supporting dissident movements, are sometimes undertaken in adversarial nations.[82]

---

81. Commission on CIA Activities Within the United States, *Report to the President* (New York: Manor Books, 1975), p. 240.

82. Roy Godson, *Dirty Tricks or Trump Cards: U.S. Covert Action and Counterintelligence* (Washington, D.C.: Brassey's, 1995).

— CHAPTER SIX —

Societal Impacts

ROLE IN SOCIAL CONTROL

In examining the societal impacts of secret police forces, it is crucial to critically analyze their role in social control, particularly within authoritarian regimes. These entities often function as formidable instruments of state power, employed to maintain control and suppress dissent.

While this chapter looks into the intricacies of secret police operations in authoritarian states and their impact on societies, it is essential to acknowledge the existence of political police units in democratic systems, such as the Special Branch in British Commonwealth countries.[83] However, it is important to recognize that the influence and operations of these units in democracies are distinctly different from their authoritarian counterparts. This difference largely stems from rigorous oversight

---

83. In Britian, Special Branch was integrated into the Counter Terrorism Command, also known as SO15, in 2006. In Australia, Special Branches operate within the police forces of various states. These units operate with a focus on counterterrorism, and other security-related matters. In New Zealand, Special Branch operates as part of the New Zealand Police, and engages in intelligence gathering and national security matters. Royal Canadian Mounted Police (RCMP) undertakes roles analogous to those of a Special Branch.

mechanisms and legislative controls inherent in democratic systems, which serve to check their powers.

Despite these controls, history has witnessed instances where political policing in democratic contexts has overstepped its bounds, notably exemplified by the FBI under J. Edgar Hoover.[84] The FBI's campaign against Dr. Martin Luther King Jr. is an example of political policing extending beyond its intended scope. This case serves as a reminder that while the focus of this chapter is on the authoritarian secret police and their pervasive influence on society's dynamics, the phenomenon of political policing is not exclusive to authoritarian states and has manifested, albeit in different forms and under different constraints, in democratic societies as well.

The nature and extent of the impact secret police have on society can be understood through several historical examples. The Soviet Union's KGB (Committee for State Security) is perhaps one of the most infamous secret police agencies. It played a crucial role in maintaining the Communist Party's grip on power through extensive surveillance, political repression, and the suppression of dissent. The KGB's activities had a profound impact on Soviet society, creating an atmosphere of fear and mistrust. People were wary of expressing dissenting opinions, and the widespread surveillance led to self-censorship and conformity.

---

84. The United States, with its distinct law enforcement and intelligence structure, does not have a direct equivalent to the Special Branch as known in Commonwealth countries. Instead, the Federal Bureau of Investigation performs roles similar to those of the Special Branch.

Another example is the Stasi, the official state security service of the German Democratic Republic (East Germany). The Stasi was known for its extensive network of informants, estimated to have encompassed a significant proportion of the population. This network enabled the Stasi to penetrate deeply into the fabric of daily life, creating a society where neighbors, friends, and even family members could be informants. The psychological impact of this pervasive surveillance was significant, breeding an environment of paranoia and distrust that undermined social cohesion.

In Latin America, during the Cold War era, secret police played a pivotal role in the so-called "Dirty Wars."[85] In countries like Argentina and Chile, these organizations were involved in the suppression of political opponents through tactics such as enforced disappearances, torture, and extrajudicial killings. The actions of these secret police forces had a lasting impact on the social fabric of these nations, leaving a legacy of trauma and a fractured society struggling with issues of justice and reconciliation.

---

85. The "Dirty Wars" refer to a period of state terrorism in Latin America, particularly in Argentina (1976–1983), characterized by military coups, repressive regimes, and human rights abuses of left-wing activists. This era saw the widespread abduction, torture, and killing of political opponents, with tactics such as enforced disappearances. Victims, often termed "the disappeared," were typically detained secretly, tortured, and killed. The Dirty Wars, part of a broader Operation Condor in South America (Argentina, Bolivia, Brazil, Chile, Paraguay, and Uruguay, with Ecuador and Peru joining later), had U.S. support during the Cold War. The legacy of these events includes ongoing judicial processes and societal efforts to address the traumas and injustices that occurred.

The Gestapo, the official secret police of Nazi Germany, is another instructive example. It became a symbol of state terror during the Second World War, responsible for enforcing Nazi ideology and eliminating opposition. The Gestapo's use of surveillance, arbitrary arrests, and torture had a chilling effect on German society, effectively silencing opposition and consolidating the Nazi regime's power.

PSYCHOLOGICAL IMPACT ON SOCIETY

One of the most significant psychological impacts is cultivating a culture of fear. The unpredictable nature of secret police activities, often characterized by arbitrary arrests, surveillance, and the absence of legal safeguards, creates an atmosphere where individuals are constantly apprehensive about their actions, words, and even thoughts. This is exemplified in the case of the Soviet Union under the KGB's surveillance. The fear of attracting the attention of the KGB led people to avoid discussing sensitive or political topics, even within the privacy of their homes, for fear of informants or wiretaps.[86]

Similarly, the Stasi in East Germany created an environment where trust was a scarce commodity. With a vast network of informants, people were unsure whom they could trust. This uncertainty permeated all levels of

---

86. One of the reasons for the reluctance to discuss political topics was the network of informants that the KGB maintained. These informants, often ordinary citizens, were recruited or coerced into reporting on the activities and conversations of their friends, family, and neighbors. The widespread presence of these informants meant that any conversation, no matter how private it seemed, could potentially be reported to the authorities.

society, from professional relationships to intimate friendships and even familial bonds. The psychological toll of such an environment was immense, leading to a breakdown in the foundation of trust in social relationships.

In Latin America, during the military dictatorships, the fear instilled by secret police forces like Argentina's National Intelligence Directorate (DINA) led to a phenomenon known as "self-censorship." People would refrain from expressing their views, discussing politics, or engaging in any activity construed as oppositional.[87] This self-imposed silence directly resulted from the fear of reprisal, detention, or worse. The psychological impact of this self-censorship was a society where open dialogue and dissent were stifled, leading to a form of collective paralysis.

The Gestapo's role in Nazi Germany further highlights how secret police can instill a culture of suspicion. The Gestapo's methods of encouraging people to inform one another, including close friends and family members, created a society where trust was eroded, and suspicion became a common social currency. The long-term psychological effects of such a climate include a deep-seated mistrust that can persist even after the fall of the oppressive regime.

GENDER AND MINORITY PERSPECTIVES

The actions of secret police often have disproportionately adverse effects on women and minority communities, highlighting a critical aspect of their societal impact. The

---

87. The fear that a trusted confidant might be an informant creats an atmosphere of paranoia and mistrust, leading many to self-censor to avoid any potential repercussions.

targeting and treatment of these groups by secret police forces not only reflect broader societal inequalities but also exacerbate them, leading to profound and lasting consequences.

Women, in many instances, have been uniquely and severely impacted by the actions of secret police. In authoritarian regimes, women who are perceived as political dissidents or as associated with opposition movements are often subjected to gender-specific forms of violence and intimidation, including sexual violence.[88] This was evident in Latin America during military dictatorships, where women political prisoners were often subjected to sexual abuse and torture. The psychological impact of such targeted violence on women is profound, affecting not only the individuals directly involved but also serving as a mechanism of broader social control through the propagation of fear.

In the context of minority communities, secret police actions often exacerbate existing social and ethnic tensions. Minority groups are frequently subject to heightened surveillance and repression, as they are

---

88. This phenomenon is not merely a byproduct of broader oppressive policies but rather a deliberate tactic employed to exploit societal gender norms and exert control. The targeting of women in such a manner serves multiple purposes: it aims to silence and punish the individuals involved, instills fear in wider society, and seeks to undermine the social fabric by turning the very identity of womanhood into a vessel of political intimidation. This gendered aspect of state repression reflects a deeper intertwining of patriarchal structures with authoritarian power dynamics, making it a critical area of analysis in understanding the full scope of secret police operations. See, for example, Claire Renzetti, *Feminist Criminology* (London: Routledge, 2013).

perceived as potential threats to the state's homogeneity and authority. For example, during the Stalinist era in the Soviet Union, ethnic minorities were often targeted by the NKVD (the precursor to the KGB), leading to mass deportations and repression. This not only inflicted immediate harm on these communities but also deepened societal divisions and mistrust between different ethnic and social groups.

Within the secret police organizations themselves, women and minorities often face significant challenges. Their representation in these institutions is typically low, and when present, they frequently encounter systemic barriers, discrimination, and limited opportunities for advancement.[89] This is compounded by the traditionally masculine and often ethnocentric culture within these organizations, which further marginalizes women and minority members. The challenges they face are not only career-related but also ethical as they navigate the complexities of being part of an organization that may be oppressing their communities or gender.

Furthermore, the roles women and minorities play within secret police forces can be complex. In some instances, they have been used in specific roles that exploit

---

89. The low representation of these groups within secret police forces is not merely a matter of numbers; it signifies a deeper entrenchment of traditional power structures and hegemonic norms. Moreover, the presence of systemic barriers serves to perpetuate a homogeneity of perspective and approach within these organizations, which can have profound implications for their operations and tactics. This dynamic also underscores a paradox: organizations tasked with surveillance and control of a diverse populace themselves lack diversity in their ranks, potentially leading to a myopic understanding and approach to their mandate.

their gender or ethnic identity. For instance, women might be employed in surveillance or interrogation roles where they are believed to be more effective or less conspicuous. However, this involvement does not necessarily translate into empowerment within the organization, as their roles are often shaped by and reinforce existing gender stereotypes and power dynamics.

RESISTANCE AND OPPOSITION

Resistance and opposition against the activities of secret police have taken various forms, reflecting the adaptability and resilience of human societies in the face of repression. From public protests to covert political activism, these forms of resistance have often played a crucial role in challenging authoritarian regimes, eventually contributing to their transformation or downfall.

Public protests have been a visible and potent form of resistance. They serve as a collective expression of dissent and a direct challenge to the authority of the state and its secret police apparatus. An example of this can be seen in the protests against the Stasi in East Germany during the late 1980s. These protests were part of a broader movement that eventually led to the Berlin Wall's fall and Germany's reunification.[90] Despite the risks of

---

90. These protests symbolized not just a collective expression of dissent but also a direct confrontation with the mechanisms of state control, exemplified by the secret police. These events illustrate the potential of public demonstrations to challenge entrenched power structures and mobilize widespread support for transformative change. Thus, the East German case provides a reference point in understanding the impact of public protests on authoritarian regimes, highlighting the interplay between grassroots mobilization and macro-political shifts.

surveillance and repression, the sheer number of people participating in these protests made it increasingly difficult for the Stasi to maintain control, signaling the weakening grip of the regime.

Political activism, often conducted in more covert forms, has also been a key strategy in resisting secret police forces. Underground networks, samizdat (self-published) literature, and clandestine meetings were some of the tactics used by dissidents in the Soviet Union to spread information and organize resistance against the KGB. Despite the risks of arrest and imprisonment, these activists played a critical role in keeping the spirit of opposition alive and creating international awareness about human rights abuses in the Soviet Union.

In Latin America, during the era of military dictatorships, human rights groups emerged as a form of resistance against the repressive actions of secret police. Organizations like the Mothers of the Plaza de Mayo in Argentina[91] brought international attention to the issue of enforced disappearances and the broader abuses of the regime. Their persistent and nonviolent resistance, often in the face of personal danger, was instrumental in highlighting the atrocities of the dictatorship and galvanizing international support for their cause.

The effectiveness of these opposition efforts varied depending on the regime's context and nature. In some

---

91. Originating as a response to the enforced disappearances during Argentina's Dirty War, this organization comprises mothers who bravely challenged the authoritarian regime by demanding information about their missing children. Their persistent protests in the Plaza de Mayo, the main square in Buenos Aires, symbolized a stand against state terrorism and the clandestine tactics of the secret police.

cases, such as East Germany, the combination of internal resistance and external pressure led to a relatively swift collapse of the regime. In other contexts, like the Soviet Union, resistance contributed to a longer-term political and social change process.

One of the factors influencing the effectiveness of resistance movements has been the ability to mobilize broad segments of society and gain international support. The Arab Spring, a series of anti-government protests, uprisings, and armed rebellions that spread across much of the Arab world in the early 2010s, exemplifies the statement that the effectiveness of resistance movements is significantly influenced by their ability to mobilize broad segments of society and gain international support.

At the core of the Arab Spring were demands for more democratic governance, economic opportunity, and human rights.[92] These issues resonated across various social, economic, and age groups in the Arab world. This widespread resonance was crucial for mobilizing large segments of the population.

In countries like Tunisia, Egypt, and Libya, the protests were not limited to a particular demographic or political group but included a broad cross-section of society. Young people, in particular, played a pivotal role, often using social media to organize protests and disseminate information, thus bypassing traditional state-controlled media channels.

The ability to mobilize such diverse groups was a factor in the initial success of these movements. In Tunisia, for example, the protests led to the ousting of President Zine

92. These issues found a profound resonance across diverse social, economic, and age groups within the Arab societies.

El Abidine Ben Ali, while in Egypt, Hosni Mubarak was forced to resign. The broad base of these movements made it more challenging for the governments to suppress them without risking further outrage and escalation.

International support also played a critical role in the Arab Spring. The global media coverage of the protests, often fueled by social media and citizen journalism, brought international attention and sympathy to the protesters' cause. This attention pressured regional governments, foreign governments, and international organizations to respond. This international focus sometimes led to direct intervention, as in Libya, where a NATO-led coalition intervened militarily.[93] In other cases, diplomatic and economic pressure was applied to the governments.

---

93. The case of Libya is an illustration of how internal political turmoil can escalate into an international crisis, involving external powers and altering the trajectory of a dictatorship that relied on a political police forces to supress desent.

— CHAPTER SEVEN —

Repercussions

PUBLIC PERCEPTION AND CULTURE

The portrayal of secret police in media, literature, and folklore often mirrors these organizations' complex and multifaceted nature and impact on society. These portrayals range from sinister and oppressive to occasionally heroic, depending on the cultural context and the historical period. The depiction of secret police in various forms of media significantly influences public perception and can shape societal trust in governance systems.

In literature, secret police have often been depicted as shadowy, omnipresent forces controlling society. George Orwell's *1984* is a seminal example where the "Thought Police" symbolized the ultimate intrusion of the state into personal freedom and privacy.[94] Such dystopian portrayals underscore the potential for abuse of power by secret police and the resulting impact on individual autonomy and societal dynamics. They also reflect and amplify public fears about state surveillance and control,

---

94. In this dystopian novel, the Thought Police embody the extreme intrusion of the state into the realms of personal freedom and privacy. Orwell's conceptualization of an omnipresent force that monitors not only actions but also thoughts and emotions serves as a powerful metaphor for the reach of authoritarian control.

contributing to a culture of mistrust towards government institutions.

In film and television, portrayals of secret police have ranged from gritty, realistic depictions to more stylized and dramatic interpretations. These portrayals often highlight the moral ambiguities and ethical dilemmas faced by individuals within these organizations, as well as the impact of their actions on the broader society. For instance, movies like "The Lives of Others," which depicts the surveillance activities of the Stasi in East Germany, offer insights into the human aspects of secret police operations, including the toll on both the surveilled and the surveillers.[95] Such narratives can foster a deeper understanding of these organizations' complex nature and societal implications.

Folklore and popular culture in regions that have experienced oppressive regimes often reflect collective memories and societal attitudes towards secret police. These narratives can be cautionary tales, satirical expressions, or symbolic representations of resistance. They process collective trauma, preserve historical memory, and reinforce societal values opposing state repression.

The impact of these portrayals on societal perceptions and trust in governance systems is significant. They can reinforce public awareness of the potential for abuse in centralized power structures and the importance of safeguards like transparency, accountability, and the rule

---

95. This movie looks at the workings of the East German secret police and its monitoring of citizens, encapsulating the psychological and moral impacts under a repressive regime where personal privacy is compromised, and trust is a rarity.

of law. In societies with a history of secret police activity, these portrayals can contribute to a persistent sense of wariness towards government institutions, impacting the public's engagement with and trust in these entities.

Conversely, in some cases, portrayals of secret police can also serve propagandistic purposes, glorifying state power and surveillance as necessary for national security or public order. In such contexts, media and literature might be used to legitimize the actions of secret police, thereby influencing public opinion to accept or even support their existence and activities.

ACCOUNTABILITY AND REFORM

One notable example of successful reform is the transformation of the Stasi in East Germany following the fall of the Berlin Wall. After German reunification, the Stasi was disbanded, and its files were opened to the public, allowing citizens to access their records. This move was a significant step towards transparency and accountability, facilitating a process of reckoning and reconciliation.[96] The dissolution of the Stasi and the subsequent handling of its legacy is often cited as a model

---

96. The opening of Stasi files not only served as a means of transparency and reckoning for the East German state but also as a cathartic process for individuals seeking closure or answers regarding the surveillance they experienced. This event is emblematic of the broader challenges and complexities involved in transitioning from an authoritarian regime to a more open, democratic system. It raises important questions about how societies can and should deal with the legacies of extensive state surveillance and control, as well as the moral and ethical considerations in balancing the public's right-to-know with individual privacy rights.

for how to deal with the aftermath of a secret police regime.

In contrast, the attempts to reform the KGB in the post-Soviet era have been met with mixed results. After the collapse of the Soviet Union, the KGB was reorganized and renamed, with its functions split among different agencies. However, the legacy of the KGB's influence has persisted in Russia, with some of its successor agencies maintaining considerable power and operating without transparency. This illustrates the challenge of dismantling entrenched security apparatuses in societies transitioning from authoritarian rule.

In South Africa, the transition from apartheid to democracy involved significant reform of the state's security apparatus, which had functioned as a secret police during the apartheid era. Establishing the Truth and Reconciliation Commission (TRC) was crucial in addressing past abuses and moving towards a more transparent and accountable system.[97] The TRC's process of public hearings and amnesty applications was an innovative approach to dealing with a legacy of state repression and human rights abuses.

The challenges to reforming secret police agencies are manifold. One of the primary obstacles is the resistance from within the organization, as members of the secret police often possess significant power and resources. Additionally, such organizations' profoundly ingrained

---

97. The TRC provided a public platform for victims to share their experiences and perpetrators to confess their actions. The TRC facilitated healing by acknowledging the wrongs of the past so that historical injustices could give way to a fostering of a collective move towards a just and transparent society.

culture of secrecy and lack of accountability pose a significant barrier to reform. Another challenge is the need to balance the pursuit of justice for past abuses with the practicalities of political stability and national security in the present.

Pathways to successful reform typically involve a combination of political will, legal frameworks, and public engagement. Establishing independent oversight bodies, enacting laws to ensure transparency and accountability, and engaging civil society in the reform process are critical steps. The involvement of international organizations and adherence to international human rights standards can also be supportive.

ACTIVISTS

COINTELPRO (Counter Intelligence Program),[98] under J. Edgar Hoover, came to light dramatically and unconventionally, highlighting the power of citizen action in exposing government wrongdoing. The program was revealed to the public in 1971 through a burglary conducted by a group of activists. This event marked a significant moment in the history of American civil liberties and intelligence oversight.

On the night of March 8, 1971, a group of activists, calling themselves the Citizens' Commission to Investigate the FBI, broke into a small FBI office in Media, Pennsylvania. The date was chosen as it coincided with the Muhammad Ali–Joe Frazier heavyweight boxing

---

98. Initiated in 1956 and continuing until 1971, COINTELPRO was a series of covert, and often illegal, activities conducted by the FBI aimed at surveilling, infiltrating, discrediting, and disrupting domestic political organizations deemed to be subversive.

match, assuming that the burglary would go unnoticed as people focused on the fight.

The group, consisting of professors, a daycare center worker, and other community members, had become concerned about government surveillance and the suppression of civil rights and anti-war activists. They successfully stole several documents and, upon examination, discovered that many contained references to an unknown operation named COINTELPRO.

These documents revealed a range of covert activities conducted by the FBI aimed at surveilling, infiltrating, and disrupting domestic political organizations. COINTELPRO targeted a wide range of groups, including civil rights organizations, feminist groups, socialist and communist parties, and anti-Vietnam War activists. One of the most notable targets was the civil rights movement, including leaders such as Martin Luther King Jr. The FBI used a variety of tactics, such as spreading misinformation, sowing discord within groups, conducting illegal wiretaps, and using other forms of surveillance.

The activists then sent copies of these documents to several newspapers, including *The Washington Post* and *The New York Times*. Initially, some newspapers hesitated to publish the information due to concerns about authenticity and potential legal repercussions. However, once the information was verified, it was widely published, leading to a national scandal.[99]

---

99. Additional details about COINTELPRO were subsequently acquired through the *Freedom of Information Act*, as well as through legal actions taken against the FBI. Moreover,

The public revelation of COINTELPRO's existence and unethical tactics led to an outcry. It raised questions about the FBI's abuse of power and the violation of American citizens' civil rights. The exposure of COINTELPRO eventually led to congressional inquiries, including the "Church Committee," which investigated abuses by U.S. intelligence agencies and led to reforms and greater oversight of these agencies.[100]

---

revelations also emerged from agents who voluntarily disclosed their involvement in these counterintelligence operations.

100. The Church Committee, formally known as the United States Senate Select Committee to Study Governmental Operations with Respect to Intelligence Activities, chaired by Senator Frank Church in the 1970s, represents a critical moment in the oversight of intelligence and secret police activities in the United States. This committee was tasked with investigating and evaluating the activities of various U.S. intelligence agencies, including the CIA and FBI, particularly in the context of alleged abuses of power. The Church Committee's findings revealed a range of covert operations and surveillance practices, both domestically and internationally, that raised concerns about the balance between national security and the protection of civil liberties.

ABOUT THE AUTHOR

Dr Henry (Hank) Prunckun, BSc, MSocSc, MPhil, PhD, is an Adjunct Associate Research Professor of intelligence methodologies at the Australian Graduate School of Policing and Security, Charles Sturt University, Sydney. He is a former Australian government intelligence analyst. Dr Prunckun spent much of his twenty-eight-year operational career in tactical intelligence and strategic research. He also served operationally in physical and cyber security, white-collar crime investigation, and counterterrorism.

INDEX

www.ingramcontent.com/pod-product-compliance
Lightning Source LLC
Chambersburg PA
CBHW022342280326
41934CB00006B/738